Contents

	page
Rescuers	2
Fire rescue	4
Ambulance rescue	10
Sea rescue	16
Calling 999	22
Index	24

Sounds in this book

ay (may)   ea (breathe)   ew (crew)

ey (they)   ind (kind)   ou (trousers)

oy (boy)   tion (station)   u (ambulance)

ue (rescue)   wh (when)

Rescuers

Look! Someone needs help!

This man has fallen off his bike.

Rescuers save lots of people and animals each year.

Let's find out about three different kinds of rescue: fire rescue, ambulance rescue and sea rescue.

Fire rescue

The fire-fighters' main job is to put out fires. But did you know that they also rescue people and animals?

Fire-fighters can rescue people
who get trapped in a road
crash or get stuck in snow.

When there is a fire, the fire station gets a call. The fire-fighters pull on their uniform quickly.

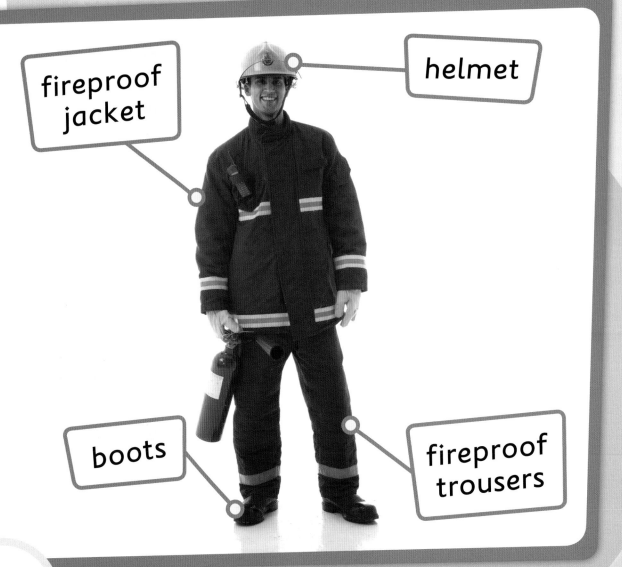

fireproof jacket

helmet

boots

fireproof trousers

The siren and flashing lights
are put on and they race
to the fire.

Look! A house is on fire!
Someone may be stuck inside.

Did you know?

Firefighters rescue over 300 people from a fire or a crash every week in the UK.

These fire-fighters are putting out the fire. Their masks help them breathe and see in the smoke.

Ambulance rescue

Sometimes people need help when they get hurt or feel ill. This boy has badly hurt his leg.

This person is very ill.

If someone is badly hurt, or very ill, it is time to call **999** for an ambulance.

Did you know?

Battersea Dogs' and Cats' Home has ambulances that rescue stray dogs and cats.

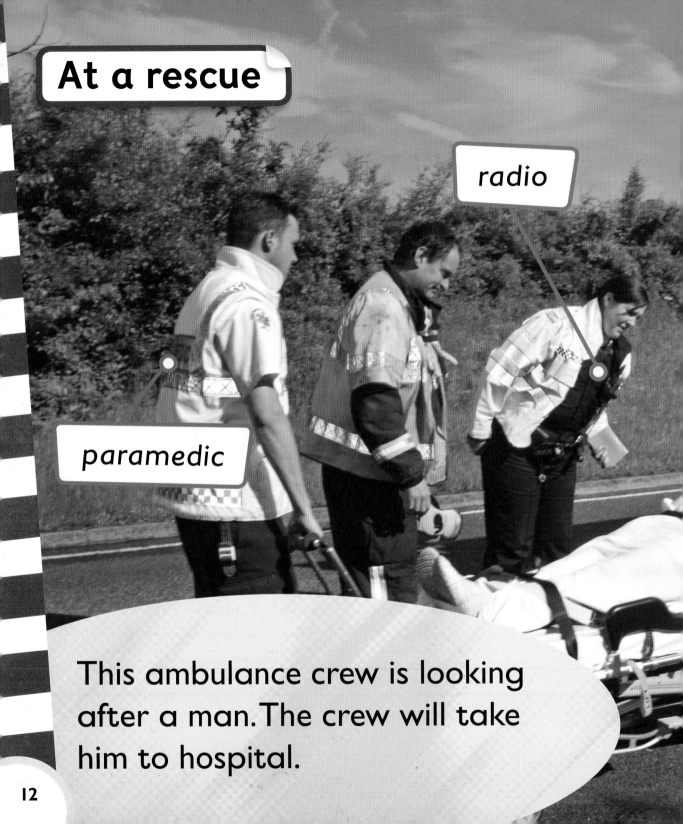

At a rescue

radio

paramedic

This ambulance crew is looking after a man. The crew will take him to hospital.

flashing lights

blanket

stretcher

13

Different sorts of ambulances come to rescue people from tricky places.

helicopter ambulance

motorbike ambulance

bicycle ambulance

boat ambulance

Which ambulance do you like best?

Sea rescue

When you go to the seaside,
you may see a beach lifeguard.
As you play or swim in the sea,
they check to see if you are safe.

The red and yellow flags
mean it is safe to swim.

Beach lifeguards sometimes use a small rescue boat to reach people.

Lifeboat rescue

A boat is sinking fast!
The crew have sent out
a call for help.

The lifeboat is rushing to the rescue to take the boat's crew safely back to land.

Did you know?

Lifeboats rescue about 21 people a day from around the UK.

Air sea rescue

This air sea rescue helicopter crew are rescuing a man in the water.

The crew send down a lifeline to the man. He grabs it, and they winch him up to the helicopter.

pilot

winch

helicopter

lifeline

rescuer

Calling 999

Call 999 if you think someone needs rescuing. If you are not sure, ask a grown up.

When you call 999:
- speak clearly
- say why you need help
- tell them the place to go to.

Never ring 999 as a joke.

Index

air sea rescue **20, 21**

ambulance **11, 12, 13, 14, 15**

bicycle ambulance **15**

boat ambulance **15**

calling 999 **22**

fire station **6**

fire-fighters **4, 5, 6, 7, 8, 9**

helicopter ambulance **14**

lifeboat **18, 19**

lifeguard **16, 17**

motorbike ambulance **14**